the john ritchie

family series

let's talk about MARRIAGE

JOHN RITCHIE LTD
=== CHRISTIAN PUBLICATIONS ===

40 Beansburn, Kilmarnock, Scotland KA3 1RH

ISBN No. 0 946351 54 6

Typeset & Print: Campsie Litho, 51 French Street, Glasgow. 0141-554 5225

Graphic Design: Graeme Hewitson

Illustrations: J. Glen

Contents

Marriage today

Of all the changes which have taken place in the second half of the twentieth century, one of the most dramatic is the attitude of men and women to the subject of marriage. The standards of past generations have been challenged and set aside. In their place we now have the modern 'enlightened' view of marriage. This view is not based on the teaching of the Bible, but on the attempts of men and women to order their lives for their own convenience, without any acknowledgement of God at all.

We are told that the only difference between a husband and wife, and a man and woman living together without being married, is a 'scrap of paper'. It is now commonly accepted that men and women will live together, and even have children, without it being felt necessary for them to marry. To be committed for a lifetime is too binding, and there is the desire to be able to end such a relationship whenever the parties involved, or even one of the parties involved, feel that it is in their own interests to do so. Even when two people do marry, the divorce laws of the day make it an easy matter to end a marriage. It is regarded like any other contract or agreement which has a 'get out clause' in it, thus encouraging many to marry without a full consideration of all the issues involved. Despite the mounting problem of single parent families, and all the other attendant hurts and heartbreaks caused by the break up of marriage and its relationship, the lessons are not learned, and the world continues on its course of setting aside what God has ordained for the ordering of society and for the benefit of mankind.

The world continues on its course of setting aside what God has ordained

So common is this state of affairs that the words 'husband' and 'wife' are now frowned upon, being replaced with the word 'partner'. Legislation and common practice make it acceptable to ignore marriage. Those who challenge these modern assumptions are seen to be old fashioned, out of step with the times, insisting on placing men and women in intolerable situations from which there is no escape.

What this approach to marriage tells us about society

All this is evidence of a society which wishes to put God out of its life. It shows that care and respect for His word has gone, and in its place there is a selfish irresponsibility. The individual now puts himself first, and what is right for him to do is what his whims or wishes dictate to him, no matter what responsibilities are ignored in pursuing this course. We live in a society which speaks much of the rights of the individual and pays only lip service to his responsibility. As a result, there is a reluctance to take the vows of marriage, because many do not wish to accept lifetime responsibility.

There is a reluctance to take the vows of marriage

The sadness in all this is that men and women are denying themselves one of the most precious gifts of God. To show selfless responsible love, and to be loved, is a major factor in living a contented, fulfilled life. The modern substitute of short term or casual relationships, and 'partnership' without the vows of marriage, robs people of the very real rewards which come to those who follow Biblical teaching on this most important aspect of life.

The attractive modern way

When referring to the subject of marriage, and relationships between men and women, the language used today is so beguiling. "Are we not masters of our own bodies?" "Do we not have the right to end 'relationships' which have broken down, and which are causing misery to both partners?" "Is it not far better to live together and have a 'loving relationship' than be bound together by a legal contract?" To the unwary it all seems to be so mature and sensible. "Is a child born out of wedlock not a true 'love child'?" "Do we not know that we change with passing years, and the person to whom we are attracted today may not be the kind of person to whom we will be attracted in years to come?" "Surely it is a fact that, if we are married and the relationship has lost its early joy, a relationship with someone else for a short time may help to put the zest back into the marriage?" These questions are asked as if the answers to them all are so obviously 'yes'. Surely marriage is to be avoided so that we will avoid all the problems which come with it!

There is very clear Biblical teaching on the subject of marriage

But the correct answer to each of these questions is an emphatic 'no'. There is very clear Biblical teaching on the subject of marriage. If we put it into practice we will find that marriage is not a strait-jacket into which we are forced, and which restricts us for the rest of our lives. It is, rather, the God-ordained way of ordering relationships between men and woman, through which love, respect and care for each other can be expressed, and enjoyed, in full measure.

Satan is always ready to suggest that what God has ordained is restrictive. He did this to Eve when he planted the thought in her mind that if she obeyed him they would "be as Gods". For her and Adam restrictions would be cast aside, and they would lead a fuller life. Human history has shown how damaging all this was, but to her initially, it proved attractive. She soon found, however, that instead of a fuller life, there was pain, heart-break and real restrictions. When the ways of God are attacked and abandoned, the alternative course, seemingly so attractive, is the road to ruin. So it is with marriage. Our society today is paying a high price for setting aside the Scriptures and adopting an approach to marriage which, rather than leading to happiness, is producing the fruit of broken lives, emotional damage, children denied the stability of united parents, and all the attendant problems which follow.

The challenge to the Christian

The challenge which faces the Christian nowadays is to show that what the Bible teaches on the subject of marriage is as valid as ever. To fall in love, to have a time of courtship nurturing respect for the Lord and for each other, and then to marry knowing that you are husband and wife until the Lord comes, or till death do you part, is still God's way. It is, therefore, still the best way.

To abandon marriage is to strike at the very core of society

When doubt is expressed as to whether the teaching of the word of God is relevant today, marriage is often cited as an example which shows how the Bible has become outmoded and unworkable in modern society. As we examine the subject we will see that not only is the Bible teaching relevant and workable today, but marriage still is the proper relationship in which men and women can find support, stability and love together. To abandon marriage is to strike at the very core of society, and leads to untold problems and heartbreak. What God ordains is always the best for us all.

Marriage is a God-ordained relationship

That marriage is a relationship which is ordained by God is clear from the Scriptures. It has not evolved over the years as man has sought to find the most suitable way of ordering society. Marriage did not develop, it was given by God. Now once we have acknowledged this basic fact we are faced with three consequences.

Firstly, man has neither right nor wisdom to change or ignore what God has ordained. We do not have the authority to introduce an alternative to marriage or even to ignore marriage completely. We do so at our peril.

Secondly, what God has ordained is always workable. He does not introduce us into a relationship which is unsuitable for our generation. If we ask if it is workable in our day, we are questioning whether what is ordained of God becomes obsolete with the passing years. No Christian would make such a claim.

Thirdly, God had only our good in view when He ordered society. Thus marriage is not a trap to ensnare us, nor is it an unworkable relationship which leads only to frustration and unhappiness. It has been given for the good and blessing of men and women.

The first husband and wife in Scripture were Adam and Eve. Their married relationship was not something which Adam dreamed up or which Eve worked to bring about. In that early marriage in Genesis 2 there is much instruction in the basic principles which should govern the relationship between a husband and wife.

What God has ordained is always workable

The Lord God said, "It is not good that the man should be alone" (v18). The animal creation had been brought into being in flocks and swarms, but man was created alone. The woman was then created that man might not be alone. Companionship is a very precious thing in life and the woman provides this for the man, as he also provides it for the woman.

Woman was created to be exactly the help which the man required

The Lord God also said, "I will make an help meet for him" (v18). The woman is not only to be the companion of the man but she is to be a helpful companion. You can have friends who are far from helpful, but this woman was to help Adam in the tasks he had been given. The onerous duties of life are better faced when you have a companion to face them with you, and provide help on the way.

It should be noted that the woman was an help who was meet for him. This means that she was suitable for him. Woman was created to be exactly the help which the man required. She was fitted completely for the task with which she had been charged. The features which mark womanhood are those which complement the features seen in manhood. They do not clash with each other, nor are they opposed to each other. The loving relationship between a husband and a wife can be a complete relationship because in the two, male and female, there has been given by God all that is required to meet the circumstances of life. Women have not gradually evolved into a sphere and role in society due to the dominating influence of men. The supposed limitations which are placed on her are not due to her ability to bear children, which are then left with her to bring up. Nothing could be further from the truth. She was created in such a way that she was fitted ideally for the task of being a help for the man and for the birth and care of children, born as a result of her relationship with her husband.

Adam did not find Eve and propose that they marry. The Lord God brings Eve to Adam. It is He who thus prompts the first marriage. That this was intended for all future generations is seen in the statement that is made in v24, that a man shall "leave his father and mother and shall cleave unto his wife". This cannot apply to Adam and Eve as no human father and mother brought them up. It indicates that marriage was intended for all succeeding generations.

Marriage was intended for all succeeding generations

**It should not
even enter the
mind of a
Christian to
contemplate
divorce**

You must observe also in this statement that marriage involves cleaving to your wife. At marriage a permanent vow is made. No one must enter marriage without the intention of living together 'until death do you part'. On this important issue let us all be quite clear. God hates divorce, or putting away, as the Scriptures also call it (Mal 2:16), and it should not even enter the mind of a Christian to contemplate divorce. Life is going to have its problems and difficulties, and there will be times when the early affection and love which you enjoyed seems to have lost its lustre. But marriage has to be worked at and not taken for granted, and a deepening love can be enjoyed by those who find that the difficulties of life can be faced together and overcome.

Clearly, therefore, marriage bears the stamp of Divine approval and we do well to guard carefully what the Lord has introduced. Marriage was not only for man in social conditions which were more primitive or are different from those which we have around us today. It has not outlived its usefulness, and it has not now to be ignored. It was given by God and has never been replaced.

Marriage must be "in the Lord"

Next to salvation, the decision to marry is the most important one which you will ever make. It is vital, therefore, that you do not make a mistake which will cause you, and others, grief for the remainder of your lives. The question of who to marry is not one that can be left solely to your emotions and feelings. There are clear guidelines in the word of God which you do well to follow closely. This issue is discussed at length in the Courtship booklet in this series, but some of the prime issues involved are worth restating here.

It is not the will of God that a believer and an unbeliever should enter into marriage. "Be ye not unequally yoked together with unbelievers" (2 Cor 6:14) clearly covers many aspects of life, one of which is the marriage bond. To be yoked together is to be committed to a common purpose, and amongst other things, an unbeliever does not share with a believer the common purpose of honouring the Lord in marriage. Do not fall into the trap of encouraging friendship with an unbeliever, confident that you can control your feelings and turn them on and off at will. What may appear to be an innocent friendship can grow until feelings become so strong on both sides that all other issues are ignored. The desire to marry becomes the dominant force, and the question of how life will be lived with one who does not know the Saviour, and has no desire to have a home where His interests are put first, is never given the serious consideration which it deserves.

To marry an unbeliever, cannot lead to a united marriage

We have known of those involved with unbelievers in this way who say that they are making this a matter of prayer, no doubt wishing to feel that they have God's approval on their actions. There is, however, no need to pray about this matter. The answer has been given to us in the Scripture which we have already quoted. To marry an unbeliever, cannot lead to a united marriage, even although he or she declares a willingness to let you continue with your spiritual life. There will be some compromise and, to keep peace in the home, you may have to neglect the gatherings of the assembly and even accompany your husband or wife to places which would not be your choice. When a family comes along, the children will find that theirs is a divided house, making the presentation of the gospel in the home all the more difficult. Remember that the blame for this unhappy situation cannot be laid at the door of the unbeliever, who has had no knowledge of the teaching of the Scriptures. It must be laid completely at the door of the believer who, knowing the Scriptures, determined to pursue a course of disobedience. Confusion and unhappiness can be caused to an unbelieving partner, after a few years of ignoring spiritual matters, when the believer starts to feel that they would like to become more active in spiritual things and to go to meetings, to enjoy the fellowship of other Christians and even to give the Lord His place in the home. This confusion and unhappiness is very understandable for the unbeliever can truly say that this was not the partner whom they married. All this is an additional strain on a marriage.

Two believers living in harmony is a relationship which God can bless

How much better it is to be able to live as we read in 1 Peter 3:7, "as heirs together of the grace of life". Two believers living in harmony is a relationship which God can bless, both looking to the day when they will enjoy the eternal relationship of which they are heirs together. This prospect which they both share adds lustre to every part of their life together. Decisions are made with eternal values in view, their home is a place where eternal principles hold good, the sorrows and sadness of life are looked at from the point of view of eternity. The relationship between husband and wife, and their love and care for each other, are all affected by this eternal bond which unites them.

Marriage must
be between two
people who share
the same
convictions and
the same values

This leads us on to a second question. Is it then scriptural to marry anyone who professes to be a believer? Once again we have to state that this is not so. Marriage must be between two people who share the same convictions and the same values. Not all believers share an interest in the study of the word of God. Not all believers enjoy the fellowship of others at conferences and other similar meetings. It is most important to ensure that both husband and wife will share the same interest in spiritual things. Can the woman respect her intended husband, knowing that he has an interest in spiritual matters and will put the teachings of the word of God into practice in their home? Does the man recognise in the woman whom he seeks to marry, spiritual qualities which are in accord with his own views?

It is easy to see the problems which will arise when a husband or wife wishes to spend free time at the week-ends attending conferences or meetings, and the other has no such desires. Put quite simply the question is, will you be in agreement in the major issues of life? The time to resolve this question is not after marriage, nor even after engagement, but before serious courtship begins.

In 1 Corinthians 7:40 we read that marriage should be "in the Lord". It should acknowledge the Lordship of Christ. This most important of decisions must therefore be the subject of prayerful consideration and a good dose of common sense. It is not enough to consider only physical attraction or intellectual agreement. The first and prime consideration is whether you are both suited to each other spiritually, and you are confident before the Lord that it is His wish for you to marry this particular person.

It is not enough
to consider only
physical
attraction or
intellectual
agreement

13

When do two people become husband and wife?

It is clear from the word of God that two people do not become husband and wife simply by setting up home together. To do so is to be guilty of fornication and shows a lack of understanding of the teaching of the Bible and of true commitment to each other. Where two people are not prepared to marry and declare their commitment for life, they must not live together. For the ordering of society, and to mark the significance of the step being taken to marry and set up a home, a marriage ceremony is necessary. Believers will be aware from the reading of Scripture that it was accepted practice for a marriage ceremony to take place. We should take note that the Lord Jesus declared His approval of such a ceremony by attending the marriage at Cana of Galilee.

At this ceremony the couple become husband and wife. They publicly declare their love for each other and their desire to be joined together in marriage. They make solemn vows to be faithful to each other, and no reason having been found for them not to be so joined, they are pronounced to be husband and wife. This is the point at which they are married. There is no stated form given in Scripture for such a ceremony, and indeed the form will differ from country to country. However a ceremony is necessary as a public declaration of the permanent commitment of both to set up home together, and to remain as husband and wife, until the Lord comes or till death do them part.

A ceremony is necessary as a public declaration of permanent commitment to remain as husband and wife

Where should such a ceremony take place? A civil ceremony, one carried out by the state, is certainly recognised, but a ceremony carried out in a local church environment is a good start to married life. There are a number of reasons for this.

At the marriage ceremony of believers there can be open

confession of the part which the Lord has had in your lives. The ceremony is a good opportunity to declare clearly that you are both saved by the grace of God. A good testimony at the beginning of married life is laying a firm foundation. There can be public commitment to acknowledge His Lordship in the years that lie ahead, in His will. You can show that the Lord who has saved you, who has brought you together and who has given you a growing love for each other, is the Lord whom you intend to serve in your married life.

Vows are taken in an atmosphere where God's word is honoured and they are therefore seen to be solemn. The vows taken on the day of marriage are serious and should not be treated lightly. Gathered round the word of God is a most suitable place to take these vows and show that you appreciate how solemn and serious they are.

At such a ceremony the teaching of the word of God regarding the truth of marriage can be declared, something which is not possible at civil ceremonies. In our current moral climate it is vital that such teaching is clearly given. The world needs to see that belief in the word of God, and practising it, is not limited to a few old fashioned people with somewhat archaic ideas, whose day has past, but involves our own younger generation too.

As was stated above, a civil ceremony is still valid and, in some cases, may be necessary and unavoidable. But how much better it is, when possible, to invite your friends and relations to gather where the Scriptures will be read, and hear the marriage vows. Even where a civil ceremony must be carried out to suit the law of the land, it is good practice to follow this with a gathering round the Scriptures in the company of your guests. What a privilege it was to have the Lord present at Cana. We do not know the identity of the two people who commenced married life on that day, but they had a wedding day which they never would forget.

Marriage is a loving relationship

Love is a vital ingredient in marriage. If we listen to what the world has to say, we will be told that love is a feeling which comes of its own accord and is sustained by itself. Should love die, we cannot be held responsible for that taking place. Love, we are told, comes, flourishes and dies beyond our control. It is a force which cannot be directed or contained and therefore this is an excuse for any conduct which is immoral and irresponsible. Thus the break up of a marriage is often justified by the fact that one of the parties now 'loves' someone else. Unfaithfulness in marriage is often justified by the same thing, that 'love' came in and the parties involved could not control this feeling. There was, therefore, an inevitability about what took place! 'Love' as the world understands it, is mainly a physical feeling, and the media constantly bombard us with what is called 'the language of love' which is essentially the language of lust. Is true love really like this? Are we so completely at the mercy of it that we cannot be held responsible for our actions?

> **The break up of a marriage is often justified by the fact that one of the parties now 'loves' someone else**

We are better to turn to the word of God. What do we find regarding the love which will exist between a husband and wife who are seeking to put the Scriptures into practice in their lives? Let us look at what the Bible has to say.

Love is selfless

In Ephesians 5:25 we read: "Husbands, love your wives, even as Christ also loved the church". The word used here for love is *agape*, which describes divine love, the love which God had for us. This is selfless love which always puts the interests of the other first. Thus the husband and the wife will not speak about and pursue their 'rights', but each will see that the well-being of the other is top of their list of priorities. Both are selfless in their care for each other. Where, on the other hand, husband and wife are selfish and pursue only what suits them, each with little or no regard for the other, there is a recipe for unhappiness, constantly pulling in different directions, no attempt being made to understand the views and the problems of each other. Selfishness breeds unhappiness, not only for others, but also for yourself.

Love always puts the interests of the other first

Love is causeless

The love of God is causeless love. We did nothing to deserve it. Similarly, in marriage, love must be shown no matter what the response may be. There will be times when the pressures and worries of life, or even the thoughtlessness which we so often display, result in us not showing the love which we feel. If you find this happening to you, do not retaliate by withholding your love in return, or by ignoring each other. You continue to display your love despite any apparent lack of response.

Sometimes such as when children are small and especially demanding, a husband may feel that he no longer receives a loving response from his wife. Similarly a wife may feel that her husband, occupied with commitments and worries of work, has no time to spare for her. As married life continues, such strains and pressures of life will need to be faced. This can lead to times when that early love which you both enjoyed will seem to be a very distant memory. It may be that the pattern of life becomes a dull routine which threatens to drain love from the relationship. This pit-fall has to be avoided. You must be constantly aware of the danger and ready to ensure that your love is displayed sincerely and sensitively. At times like these the best long term policy is to show that you like to express your love, no matter what the response is. This can be one of the difficult areas of marriage to handle, but if faced calmly, without resorting to recriminations or anger, the marriage bond can be strengthened.

Little acts of kindness can wonderfully bind a couple together

Love is kind

Show that you like to express your love

Another word which is used for love is *philanthropia*. This describes love which includes kindness. In Titus 3:4 wives are told to love their husbands in this way. What we have here is love which shows kindness and courtesy. It is never rude or overbearing, but always considerate in its dealings. Husbands, too, must show this kind of love. Any husband or wife who adopts an overbearing, rude attitude towards the other, is embarking on a pathway which will lead to much unhappiness for both of them.

Little acts of kindness can wonderfully bind a couple together. What about a little present occasionally, the sharing of work load in the home or taking time to enquire about each other's problems or worries? All these little acts go towards the deepening of mutual love. They indicate that you do not take your husband or wife for granted, but still appreciate all that they are and all that they do. Where kindness is shown love will deepen.

Love is physical

The Greek word *eros*, which is used of physical love, is not itself found in the word of God. Physical love, however, is present in Scripture. This love has been debased today to such an extent that the purity and joy associated with it has almost been forgotten.

There is nothing impure about physical and sexual love between husband and wife. We read in Hebrews 13:4 that "Marriage is honourable in all things, and the bed is undefiled". Physical love has been ordained and created by God for the mutual satisfaction of husband and wife. It is the responsibility of both to provide selflessly for the other in this way. When two people love each other, this most intimate of human relationships is a pure and holy way of displaying that love.

In this love there will be deep mutual care and consideration for each other, but there must never be a selfish withholding of physical love from one another. An important passage of Scripture to consider is 1 Corinthians 7:3-5.

Sexual relationships are only permitted within marriage

"Let the husband render unto the wife due benevolence; and likewise also the wife unto the husband. The wife hath not power of her own body, but the husband: and likewise also the husband hath not power of his own body but the wife. Defraud ye not one another, except it be with consent for a time, that ye may give yourselves to fasting and prayer; that Satan tempt you not for you incontinency."

Abstinence from physical love in marriage should only be with the agreement of both husband and wife, for a specified period of time, and only for the purpose of promoting prayer and spiritual exercise. A marriage which drifts into a situation where there is no physical expression of love is one which is in great danger.

Another lesson which we learn from these verses in 1 Corinthians 7 is that the husband and wife do not have sole rights over their own bodies. The husband has a claim on his wife and the wife has a claim on her husband. Often today we hear people saying that 'it is my body to do with as I like'. This is untrue on two grounds. It denies the right which God has (1 Cor 6:20), and it denies the right which a husband or wife has (1Cor 7:4).

Sexual relationships are only permitted within marriage. God never intended that such relationships should be short term or casual affairs, merely for the gratification of physical lust. Impure sexual behaviour of any kind is sinning against your own body. In the Ten Commandments the instruction is clear, "Do not commit adultery", and believers are warned that their bodies are the temple of the Holy Spirit (1 Cor 6:19). Thus the gravity of immoral conduct is emphasised to us. Quite apart from the important question of how it affects our relationship to the Lord, impure and immoral behaviour also shows a complete disregard for the rights and well-being of a husband or wife. Faithfulness, therefore, is a must!

Faithfulness, is a must!

19

In the expression of physical love between husband and wife, however, proper fulfilment and joy will be experienced by those who do not act simply to satisfy their own feelings, but who do so to satisfy the feelings and needs of their partner. Thus, as both seek to satisfy the other, with each deeply expressing and giving love to the other, there will be true mutual fulfilment. In marriage husband and wife satisfy their mutual physical needs because of their love for each other.

Love is patterned on the love of Christ

When we read in Ephesians 5:23-29, Paul describes the love which a husband must have for his wife. Let us examine this, careful to note that this love should bear the character of the love which the Lord Jesus has for the church. In v25 husbands are exhorted to love their wives even as Christ also loved the church. In v29 a husband has to love his wife as himself, even as the Lord nourishes and cherishes the church. Love which finds expression in so many different ways, comes to its full blossom when it is patterned on the love which the Lord Jesus has for the church. Keep Him before you, honouring Him in your marriage, and you will be able to enjoy love to the full.

Keep Him before you, honouring Him in your marriage

The responsibilities of a husband

Everything introduced by God is orderly, and in Scripture we find the duties and responsibilities of husbands and wives set out clearly. The husband undertakes to care for and support his wife in the following ways.

The husband accepts responsibility

"Therefore shall a man leave his father and his mother, and shall cleave unto his wife: and they shall be one flesh" (Gen 2:24).

In this verse we have the first definition of marriage in Scripture. When marriage takes place a man leaves his father and his mother and establishes a new home of which he is the head. At this stage he accepts the responsibilities of marriage and of the care of his wife. Any man who wishes to avoid such a responsibility should not marry, as he is not ready to become a husband. This would indicate to us that the bridegroom should be of an age and maturity where he is able to take on such responsibilities. It does not mean that age limits are set before which marriage cannot take place, but it does indicate how unwise it would be to rush into marriage at an age where it is not possible to provide for a wife the basic necessities of life. In our modern society it is usual for the bride and the bridegroom to contribute to the setting up of a home. Where the couple cannot support themselves, marriage is not to be recommended. The discipline of saving for and planning a home for your life together, is an important part of character development, and teaches values which will stand you in good stead in the years ahead.

Any man who wishes to avoid responsibility should not marry

The responsibility to lead

"The husband is the head of the wife, even as Christ is the head of the church" (Eph 5:23).

As the head of his wife the first responsibility of a husband is to lead. He has to provide her with loving, spiritual leadership and to ensure that the spiritual tone of the marriage and the home is maintained. In order to fulfil this role the husband must live in such a way that he is respected by his wife, who will accept his leadership because of the consistency of his own life and example. This does not necessarily mean that the husband will be more spiritual than the wife, but he will provide leadership in the home which will be lovingly respected.

The husband will lead in setting the spiritual atmosphere of the home. He will pray with the family, and as they watch how he lives, they will see that he loves the Lord and His word. He will be seen to have an interest in the gatherings of the local church and to be present at these gatherings whenever possible. When decisions have to be made he will take part in the discussions on all the issues involved, but ultimately he will bear the responsibility for whatever decision is made. He is really a poor husband who refuses to make a difficult decision, and then blames his wife if the decision which she was left to take is seen, in retrospect, to be wrong.

None of us knows what kind of adults our children will turn into

When a husband fails to give direction, but lives to himself, with little concern for the spiritual well being of his wife and family, he is denying them the privileges of having a christian husband and father as an example. None of us knows what kind of adults our children will turn into, but if you have given them no example, you cannot complain when they also neglect spiritual things. It is true that a good spiritual family atmosphere is no guarantee that children will be the kind of adults you would like them to be, but if you have lived Christ before them you know that you have fulfilled your responsibility.

A teenager will soon appreciate the irony of a father reprimanding him for lack of interest in gatherings of the local church and the word of God, if the father has shown scant regard to these in times past. Families are quick to spot inconsistencies in the lives of their parents. One fact which you should always keep before you is that young children appreciate and remember much more than you imagine. It is folly to think that, while the children are young, you do not need to give this good spiritual example, and propose only to change your ways when they become older. They will soon let you know if you wish them to live a life which you have not lived yourself. As a husband and father you must be an example from the beginning.

Families are quick to spot inconsistencies in the lives of their parents

The responsibility to love

"*Husbands love your wives, even as Christ also loved the church and gave Himself for it*" (Eph 5:25).

As well as the responsibility to lead we now see that a husband has a responsibility to love. Some of the issues involved in this have already been considered, but we will now examine some facts which need to be underlined for a husband.

Love does not continue to flourish without attention. It requires a deliberate attitude on the part of a husband to keep his love for his wife clear and sharp. Thus he is exhorted to love his wife. In the early days of marriage this will be something which comes easily, but a few years later, a husband coming home to a wife who is careworn and stressed after a day spent with their noisy, active children may wonder where his smart, well-groomed young bride has gone! It is at such times that he

23

must show that he loves his wife as much as ever. How, then does he show this love?

His love must, first of all, be a sacrificial love, like that of Christ who loved the church and gave Himself for it. He displayed His love by sacrificing Himself, and so must a husband. In practical terms this means that he must always put the needs of his wife before his own. In the situation just described he will be willing to help with the children and the tidying up, rather than relax and put his feet up! There is ample opportunity to do this in other ways too in the early years of marriage when budgets may be tight and little cash is to spare. When, for example, a husband and wife both need an item of clothing, and there is money available for only one of them, the spiritual husband will put the need of his wife first, and be prepared to wait a little longer to purchase what he requires. He is seen to be unselfish, and this will not only confirm to his wife how he loves her, but will also enhance his moral right to give guidance in the home. One who sacrifices for others is worth listening to. A husband, however, who looks after his own interests first and displays little regard to the needs of wife and family is clearly not loving his wife "as Christ also loved the church".

When we speak of the husband being the head of the wife some may consider this to be a privileged position which gives him rights which are denied to his wife. Some husbands may think, quite wrongly, that this gives them the right to treat their wife as being inferior. This is far from what the Bible teaches! Sacrifice is the first

responsibility of headship. The spiritual husband considers his wife first, and the husband who denies this is living in disobedience to Scripture.

A husband's love must also be directed to the spiritual welfare of his wife. The Lord gave Himself for the church that He might sanctify and cleanse it with the washing of water by the Word. Thus the Lord had in view the spiritual well being of the local church. A husband will always keep before him the spiritual needs of his wife. He will ensure that she is able to attend the gatherings of the local church as regularly as he can. Once children are born he will take his turn at remaining in the house to enable his wife to attend the gatherings for prayer, for Bible teaching and for the Breaking of Bread. He will ensure that his home life is ordered in such a way that his wife can retain a spiritual life of her own. Does she have time to read and pray, does he encourage her to talk of spiritual matters, and does he encourage her to live in a way which is pleasing to the Lord, never making demands on her which are contrary to Scripture? A wife who can never be free to have fellowship with other believers, and who is constantly tied to the house because of the thoughtlessness or selfishness of her husband, is in danger of losing her appetite for spiritual things.

The love of a husband for a wife must be as strong as the love which he has for himself, for men ought to love their wives as their own bodies (Eph 5:28). We read much today of the need for husband and wives to have a fifty-fifty relationship in everything. Marriage, however, demands much more than that. In this, the husband's side, we have learned that he has to give all for his wife, and to love her and care for her as he would care for himself. The husband is head of the wife, but as the head he puts his wife first and he loves her totally. The standard is high, but this is what is taught in Scripture, and is the pattern to which we must all conform.

> **The love of a husband for a wife must be as strong as the love which he has for himself**

The responsibility to labour

"No man ever yet hated his own flesh; but nourisheth and cherisheth it, even as the Lord the church" (Eph 5:29).

The third responsibility faced by a husband is the responsibility to labour. The purpose of this labour is to nourish, by the provision of the necessary food, and to cherish by the provision of necessary warmth. Thus he must feed, clothe and house his wife and family. In our present day it has become the practice for both husbands and wives to work, but we must not lose sight of the fact that it falls to the husband to provide for his wife. It is true that illness may force a husband to cease employment, or that the scourge of unemployment may make it impossible for him to be employed as he would desire. However, where conditions prevail which make it possible for a man to have employment, it is his responsibility to provide for his wife. Certain practices today are contrary to Scripture, such as the concept of a man willingly leaving his employment to tend the home and family while his wife works. It may be that this is done because the earning power of the wife is greater than that of the husband, but this is no excuse for setting aside the order of the word of God. The 'house husband' is taking the wife's place and the woman is taking the man's place. How can such a man lead and guide the house as the head of the wife?

The caring husband will ensure that he and his wife do not load themselves with financial commitments which are so onerous that his wife must work, even when their children are born, and be unable to fulfil her role as a wife and mother.

Peter's advice to husbands

"Likewise, ye husbands, dwell with them according to knowledge, giving honour unto the wife, as unto the weaker vessel, and as being heirs together of the grace of life; that your prayers be not hindered" (1 Peter 3:7).

We know that Peter was a married man and that his mother-in-law lived in the same house as did Peter and his wife. His advice is threefold.

(i) A husband must be spiritually intelligent.

The husband will dwell with his wife according to knowledge. He will have an intelligent appreciation of what marriage is and will put this into practice. It is sad to see a husband who is less spiritually aware and intelligent than his wife.

(ii) A husband will honour his wife.

He will treat her as the weaker vessel, not weaker in intelligence or understanding, but weaker physically. He will not abuse her in any way and will treat her with the dignity and respect which her honoured position demands. She is not a servant to be ordered about as if she had no rights. The head of the wife is not the dictator over the wife.

(iii)   A husband will recognise the unity which exists between them.

As believers they will live together, sharing the joys and sorrows of life, but looking forward to that day when they will enjoy a relationship which is eternal and which is greater than anything which they enjoy now. They are heirs together of the grace of life.

As the head of the wife it would be so easy for the husband to misuse the place which he has and to regard himself as being superior to his wife. This will not only cause much pain and suffering in the home, but will also lead to the wife losing all respect for her husband. In the long run he will be the loser. If, however, he lives as Scripture teaches, loving and honouring his wife, putting her first at all times, and striving to meet her needs, ensuring that the Lord has the first place, there can be a happy, successful marriage, the joys of which grow with the passing years.

The responsibilities of a wife

Having looked at the responsibilities of a husband we now turn to the responsibilities of a wife. These are of a different nature and they complement those which belong to the husband.

A wife will submit to her husband

Modern society is most uncomfortable with this fact. The marriage of today is said to be one of equals who have the same roles and the same parts to play. The fact that a woman gives birth to children is seen as nothing more than an inconvenient biological matter which can be easily overcome. If, however, as we have seen, the husband is the head of the wife, the wife is subject to her husband.

"Wives, submit yourselves unto your own husbands, as unto the Lord" (Eph 5:22).

Submission acknowledges the Lordship of Christ. The submission of a wife to a husband is ultimately the acknowledgement of the Lordship of Christ. After writing the above verse Paul states that the head of the wife is the husband even as Christ is head of the church. The spiritual wife sees that her submission is not simply the question of the relationship between her and her husband, but it goes far beyond her home. In 1 Corinthians 11:3 we learn that the head of the woman is the man, the head of the man is Christ and the head of Christ is God. This is God's order in creation and cannot be altered. He has ordained that authority over the woman rests with the man, just as authority over the man rests with Christ. Thus the woman sees that she is part of this great relationship which has God at its head. She will be honoured, as will be the man, to have part in such a relationship. As a wife she will acknowledge this and assist her husband in setting the tone of the spiritual quality of their home and their relationship.

The woman sees that she is part of this great relationship which has God at its head

"Wives, submit yourselves unto your own husbands, as it is fit in the Lord" (Col 3:18).

Submission fulfils a spiritual obligation. The submission of a wife to a husband is not an optional extra in marriage. This verse from Colossians tells us that it is fit in the Lord. This means that it is a fitting and proper thing to do and is an obligation on all, declaring as it does, the Lordship of Christ. There is little point in a wife seeking to display all the signs of piety if it is known that her husband is not head of his own home. A determined wife can exert power over her husband in many different ways, and use that power to ensure that her wishes are always carried, no matter what her husband decides. A wife can undermine the confidence of her husband by always comparing him to others in an unfavourable light. She can complain whenever he decides on anything, so that if asked outside of the home to undertake some task, he is afraid to take the news home, knowing what the response will be. It is also possible for a wife to refuse the physical relationship of marriage in order to have her wishes met. None of this is honouring to the Lord and shows that she has no respect for her husband.

A determined wife can exert power over her husband in many different ways

"Likewise ye wives, be in subjection to your own husbands; that if any obey not the word, they also may without the word be won by the conversation of the wives" (1 Peter 3:1).

Submission shows a good example. In a home where the wife has been saved, but the husband remains an unbeliever, there may be difficulties. There is the temptation on the part of the wife to preach constantly at her husband until he becomes wearied. Peter teaches us here that there is a much more effective way of showing what it means to be a Christian. The wife submits herself to her husband, and shows by her manner of life, the attractiveness of being a follower of Jesus Christ. If he is won, it will be by godly living and not by nagging and preaching constantly, or taking every opportunity to turn the conversation round to spiritual things.

A wife will supervise the home

"I will therefore that the younger women marry, bear children, guide the house, give none occasion to the adversary to speak reproachfully" (1 Timothy 5:14).

It is the prime responsibility of the wife to care for the home and to bring up children

The home is the place of her spiritual responsibility. We saw in our consideration of the husband's responsibilities that it fell to him to provide for his wife. In like manner it is the prime responsibility of the wife to care for the home and to bring up children. In this way there is a real division of labour in the home, with clear guidelines as to the different areas of responsibility.

It must never be thought that the work of a housewife is a demeaning, unfulfilling role. When Paul wrote that the younger women should guide the house he was speaking of the guidance and direction of a

home. He was using a term which denoted mature, dignified responsibility. The wife is the 'house manager' under whose control the house functions smoothly. The husband can safely leave to her the budgeting for the home and the organisation of the home. Into her care is committed the children who have been given to them by the Lord.

Today such a role is looked on with distaste by many wives who see being a housewife as a second rate, servant-like way of life. The husband is at work fulfilling himself in the pursuit of his career, while she is left at home in a situation which has no feeling of fulfilment in it. She considers that life is passing her by, and to her is left the boring, tedious, part of marriage. If she could combine this role with a career there would be more money around to meet their needs and she would be able to find achievement, fulfilment and satisfaction outside of her home. This would make her a more lively and interesting wife, and would enable her to have a fuller life.

It sounds so appealing and logical, providing more finance for the family and rewarding her with added self esteem. But is it really like that? The prime responsibility of the wife, according to the word of God, is to carry out the vital and most important task of managing the home and bringing up the children. Any other way of life which compromises her ability to do this is not what a spiritual wife would desire. It is true that there are financial pressures in our modern society and it is now accepted practice that a wife will work and, if necessary, employ a baby-minder to take care of the children when she is at work. It must be emphasised, however, that the bringing up of children is the responsibility of the wife, helped by her husband. It is not the responsibility of baby-minders, or even of grandparents.

Bringing up of children is not the responsibility of baby-minders, or even of grandparents

There may be circumstances, such as illness and unemployment, which make it necessary for a wife to seek employment. It may be that where there are no children she may wish to spend a few hours a day out of the home. It may be, however, that she is working simply to provide material things which are not necessary. A wife, whether she be a mother or not, can have a satisfying full-time job caring for her husband and home. If time is at her disposal she has the opportunity of using it in the furtherance of the gospel and in the many areas of help and spiritual guidance which a spiritual woman can give. She does not preach in the gatherings of the local church, but there is much else that needs to be done which is so profitable.

"She shall be saved in child bearing" (1 Tim 2:15).

The home is the place of her spiritual preservation. When Paul wrote these words he was thinking of the possibility of a woman seeking to move outside the role which God has given to her. Just as a man may seek to do this by avoiding the responsibilities he has been given, and even taking on those which are not his, so a woman can do this by seeking to assume responsibilities which are not for her.

In carrying out the work which the Lord has for her to do she will be preserved from ambitions which are not of God. When Satan tempted Eve she should have taken the matter to her husband, but she stepped outside of her role and took upon herself a course of action which she had no right to undertake without the knowledge of Adam. The spiritual wife today will recognise the dangers of declaring independence of thought and action. In the home she will be saved from this and will find her fulfilment and satisfaction in her husband and family.

A wife will seek the good of her husband

"An help meet for him" (Gen 2:20).

She is a help suitable for him. We have already considered these words from the book of Genesis, but what do they mean in practical terms for a wife? It will be a prime objective in her life to assist her husband spiritually. She will encourage him to set time aside for the study of the Scriptures. If she wishes to have a husband who is making spiritual progress she must recognise that, when he comes home from work, he will need to have time for these things. The husband will not take advantage of this by being lazy in the home, but he will appreciate the interest which his wife has in these important issues. A wife who is constantly complaining and making demands on her husband which denies him time for the Scriptures, is harming both of them.

She will be a help also in bearing a good testimony and not engaging in any activity which will cause him harm or embarrassment. A wife who engages in gossip will damage her husband's testimony as well as her own. A wife who dresses in a provocative way will not commend her husband. If she is known as a spendthrift it will also reflect badly on him. On the other hand, a wise wife will seek to act in a kind, constructive and spiritual way, and will be a real blessing and benefit to her husband.

GOSSIP!

Advice from the book of Proverbs

The writer of the book of Proverbs had much experience of the ways of the world and, as a shrewd observer of human conduct, he came to conclusions which are worth considering.

Advice to husbands

Be joyful with your wife.

"Rejoice with the wife of thy youth" (Prov 5:18).

The husband is to love only his own wife

Proverbs 5:15-20 are a lesson on the joys of faithfulness in marriage. The husband is told to drink only from his own fountain, to love only his own wife. As the years pass there is blessing in being satisfied with the wife of your youth, never to wander from her and ever to be faithful to her, even when youth has long gone. Then there can be true joy together, made deeper and fuller with the passing years.

Be faithful to your wife.

"Can a man take fire into his bosom, and his clothes not be burned?" (Prov 6:27).

There is a price to be paid for unfaithfulness and immoral conduct. The man who takes fire into his bosom will most certainly be burned, and the man who goes after the "strange woman" will eventually feel the pain of his unfaithfulness. There is a price to be **There is a price to be paid for unfaithfulness** paid for all sin, and unfaithfulness in marriage has implications which strike at the very foundations of your life. Remember what can be lost, and value what God has given you.

Be thankful for your wife.

"Whoso findeth a wife findeth a good thing, and obtaineth favour of the Lord" (Prov 18:22).

A husband must recognise the value of his wife. A true wife is more than a woman, she supports her husband, cares for him and loves him. A spiritual husband will recognise that a good wife has been given to him through the favour of the Lord, and he will be thankful to the Lord for such graciousness towards him. To see the hand of the Lord in bringing husband and wife together is a good start for any marriage. Always be thankful to the Lord for how He ordered your pathway in life.

Advice to wives

Be considerate towards your husband.

"The contentions of a wife are a continual dropping" (Prov 19:13).

A wife who is always complaining makes a misery of the life of her husband. Home becomes a place to be avoided rather than enjoyed. He will eventually 'turn off' and ignore all that his wife says. The resultant lack of communication will damage the marriage. The continual dropping of water is an irritant which gradually turns into a form of torture. So also are the words of a complaining wife. Treat your husband wisely. Constant complaints demean him and strain his love for you. Thus the next verse tells us that a prudent wife is from the Lord. Let your husband see that you, indeed, are from the Lord.

MOAN! GROAN!

Be industrious for your husband.

"She looketh well to the ways of her household" (Prov 31:27).

This closing section of the book of Proverbs has to do with the value of an industrious wife. A husband is ill-served by a wife who keeps a home which is slovenly and dirty. She is undermining him and she is limiting his usefulness. A caring wife will ensure that the house is a home into which anyone can enter, and which can be used for the work of hospitality.

Be godly before your husband.

"Favour is deceitful, and beauty is vain: but a woman that feareth the Lord, she shall be praised" (Prov 31:30).

Favour, or charm, can be deceptive, and beauty passes. What a husband requires beyond everything is a wife who fears the Lord. She will order her household in a godly way, and will provide the right environment for him to progress in spiritual matters. She will not be materialistic, always asking for what she knows will strain their resources. She will not ask him to sacrifice his spiritual life for the sake of promotion in his work, because she understands true values. Little wonder, then, that she is to be praised.

What a husband requires beyond everything is a wife who fears the Lord

35

A final word

In this booklet we have been laying out some of the basic Biblical principles which govern marriage. The prize to be gained by those who put these principles into practice is very great indeed. A firm anchor in an unsettled society is a happy home where the Lord Jesus is honoured, and where husband and wife share a mutual and growing love.

Such a home can be the prize which every Christian gains. It will not, however, simply happen of its own accord. There must be a determined effort to follow the principles of Scripture, and to turn your back on the siren calls of a godless world which promises what it cannot deliver. Ignore the tasteless literature and music of a lustful society, and make your home a place where true love is to be found.

There must be a determined effort to follow the principles of Scripture

Children born into such an environment will enjoy the great privilege of growing up under the godly influence of parents who honour the Lord and seek the salvation and the good of their family.

If your home is like this, you will enjoy the presence of the Lord, and the blessing of the Lord will be yours in the bright days and in the dark days until He comes or until death do you part.

Family life and family values are under threat more than ever before, yet the family is the one stabilising unit for all of society. So many individual, community, and national problems can be traced back to the sad disintegration of family life.

The John Ritchie family series

Of course it was God who designed the family unit for the well-being of mankind, young and old. In this series of booklets, we are taken back to the Bible to see again that God's principles are the only secure foundations for our lives.

The author, John Grant, lives in the west of Scotland with his wife Ann. They have a grown-up family of three sons and one daughter. He travels widely with an effective evangelistic and teaching ministry.

Titles in this series include

Courtship
Marriage
Marriages in Difficulty*
Children*
The Teenage Years*
Grandparents*
Giving*
The Unequal Yoke*
Further Education*
Our Leisure Time*
Bereavement*
Employment*

*These will become available at approximately three-monthly intervals

ISBN 0-946351-54-6

9 780946 351541

JOHN RITCHIE LTD
CHRISTIAN PUBLICATIONS